Last Night's Dream Corrected

Pretend Genius Press

London, New York, San Francisco, Seattle, Washington D.C.

www.pretendgenius.com

Published simultaneously in the United States and Great Britain in 2006
by Pretend Genius Press
London, New York, San Francisco, Seattle, Washington D.C.

ISBN 0-9747261-6-8

Contents

Contents

Contents

Introduction

It's not easy to put yourself into the tattered loafers of a contemporary poet. He isn't much read - not on this continent at least. He doesn't represent any kind of iconic allusion. He isn't quoted by politicians except on inauguration day or when they're reaching for what they hope is sublime, most likely in a speech they instinctively know will be too long. I can imagine Senator Throb screaming at his speech writers later to not give him the kind of material that causes the voters' eyes to glaze over. "It's the last goddam time we're quoting any goddam poetry." So what could possibly be said about the poets in this anthology that they might not have already lied about to their mothers?

Instead I'll talk about you. I try to visualize you reading this introduction and then the entire book. I can't exactly picture you, obviously, but know you're not the average reader or you wouldn't have selected this book - while I admit the cover is attractive. You either have a thirst for knowledge or, at least, elevated diversion. You're not necessarily highly educated but you ain't no dumb ass. I love you. I want to crawl up your leg a homing finger but I'm not after your libido. It's your spine from about mid-lower back up into your brain stem that I want to straighten with the gentlest of tingling. Your head should raise and your chin should point. And you should feel it in your ears.

The poets in this book share that wish. I doubt that any one of them hopes for the sentences they've crafted to be in all senses useless. They've set out to touch something, somehow, with only words at their disposal. Words can thrill, still, in this day and age, if only for a moment. There are still moments a book can energize a latent or near forgotten purpose to our lives. Maybe that is too much to hope for with this volume, but maybe hoping for an initiative sparked by one or two of these writers leading to future moments in which that is attained, isn't.

Bloog Mandrake
Seattle USA

Raewyn Alexander

speaking with Dante by the apples in produce

thunder debates with ice and lightning leads

speaking with Dante by the apples in produce

he's not recognisable as a dead famous writer
the steam coming off his feet gives him away though
and the celestial blue about his eyes
dark circles never looked like a summer sky before

somehow due to work and imagination
we both speak the same language
although we're from different places and times
and people think differently now
we adjust the way trees do to seasons
this is an age and a season of confusion

Dante also had an eon of writhing morass back there
common ground and both admiring the apples
they're green and some are red streaked with orange
although they are barely like the globes he knew
far more ideas than we know what to do with
we share a laugh about heaven and hell
since we're between worlds for a short while

and he rises gently towards the fluorescent lights
while I sashay around to the wine racks' startle
past them down to fresh mussels in their own rain
and it seems there's a bubble about me unpoppable

how did he understand what this supermarket is?
immediately perhaps it appeared a jungle full
alien flowers and fruit and new colours arranged
the drenched intensity and plethora could be hell
putting on my sunglasses I'm out through auto doors
a few words he's never heard of and this ozone stretched sun

thunder debates with ice and lightning leads

this mosh pit of weather punks the air
finding the finer places you indented speak
dark and a plink of hot water overflow
plumbers cellphones red hot and elusive

i sleepwalked into the eyes of it
drenched with what used to be promises
your dark ghost tossing new hair
insurance could cover this if it had heart

instead there's this patched memory and floods
the lift after a storm synapses a new channel
a pore of books and this chesting voice
reaching out to known strangers with my softer hands

Richard Atkinson

laughing inside the inside

laughing inside the inside

it was a cold day, drizzling, late spring.
i got my coffee and sat down.

in front of me i could see the back of a bald headed man
although not his face

having not noticed his face when i entered
i wondered if he had one
well, you never can be too sure.

a young mum, sat to the side of me with a toddler
explaining to the waitress what school
she wanted to send him to.

noticed big grey patches of moisture
on the café's front window
looking out onto the street.

and at the top of the window
the word "HEATWAVE"
of the shop opposite,
in bold black letters on red.

i clicked my camera twice.
no one appeared to notice or laugh.

i never did check if he had
a face.

Bill Berkson

But Then

A Recording Device

In Costume

But Then
  for Anselm Hollo

Nobody knows
the trouble – the wasted
whistles, catcalls, oceanic blitz,

    diehard
   push-button
fashion-conscious
   expressivity.

A Recording Device

Well, back to my ablutions then.
You never walk in the same movie
twice or feel the traction between
experience's proprietary sleepless
light pervading the girder's
                           unclouded eye.

You will want to lap the sheen off anyone's personal orifice
to imagine vapors crossing the grid's white string
                           wrapped
around a rusty nail, sweet denim moon swallowed up,
            coercing landscape lovers
                  articulated.
      Between action-packed earth
            and acquisitive skies
                  there's a job to be done:
            spatial distances
      simply minding parked cars
in suspicious places – the shrine of matter, perhaps
            ephemeral yet.

In Costume

The endangered energy guys are coming on a Monday
And the steamed-up picture window (time being what it is, its prolonged
Disconnect elaborately personified) wavers blue-ishly spotlit,
Affecting a slight concussion to face the styptic deer.

In the parlance of permanence many bulbs need replacing.
I heard the woods speaking but they went about it the wrong way around,
Panting like mutts in the leafy strata.
Unlikely lunch: Dark toast soaked in soup du jour.

Agnes Morehead, Goddess of Nimbly Erected Spite, tell us,
What is it that will make life palatable when so it is?
And lunch absorbs from light executive privilege
At the high end of the cerebral cortex afloat on my fiery palatial plank.

She flies! The saucer can't *not* act.
The clock is whole, its animations invariably tingling,
Recruited to receive pronouncement of the final
Anagram hastily received dark nights long before graduation.

J. Tyler Blue

To Tyus

To Tyus

every time we say goodbye
it seems to get harder for me
and easier for you

even if I moved next door
or in the same house
I can see that you are going to go
your own way

and do things that don't include
falling asleep in my arms
holding my hand
or asking me to get something
because it is just too high

all I can do
to delay the inevitable
is squeeze you tighter
hold you longer
take pictures of you sleeping

and store away
a million million
memories

I miss you

Sean Brijbasi

last night's dream corrected

last night's dream corrected

oh bathsheba two words of house.

her dusty feet sprinkle golden surgical openings. greta garbo is not
my sister.

a door opens and i enter like someone who—he

sits in a chair, reading a book, unaware of my theme music,
turning crispy pages back and forth, compromising passages.

greta plays with her toy boats. she uses the rug as the ocean. her
sunlight pasted above a map of the medulla oblongata.

"i have to take off my dress or the rain will stop", she says.
"yes, that is true", i say.

i follow her onto the grass, where i paint the lingo.

it is me.

but,

"beautiful" i hear. "beautiful".
"how did you do that?". "we didn't know you could".

it is unfinished.

greta, my sanguine hypothesis, your flag is an opiate dress the
marching band salutes. it is a painting of you and your country (by
this lake) the room is brighter and better for reading the lattice
pitch of children covered by folds of

happening.

it is a testament to the conceivable.

but,

"remarkable".

greta?

i can't paint.

Terri Carrion

Wandering through the big picture

When I was in love

WANDERING THROUGH THE BIG PICTURE

Everybody's a dreamer and everybody's a star
And everybody's in movies, it doesn't matter who you are"

"Celluloid Heroes", The Kinks

While watching Johnny Depp
roll around in piles of drug money,

> in the movie *Blow* (blah, blah, blah)
> she's reminded of her old friend in LA,

who one night in a parking lot
in Chinatown (blah, blah) pinned her down

> against the car seat
> shoved a tiny silver spoon up

her virgin nostril
The rest of the night (blah, blah) she spent

> moving in and out of black
> lacquered bathroom stalls

of Madame Wongs,
The Roxy and finally (blah, blah, blah)

> The Rainbow Room[1]
> on Sunset Blvd. where she

---

[1] World famous bar and grill know for Rock and Roll roots. Staff stories
include: "John Lennon fell down those stairs"…"Brett Michaels puked in that
corner"…"Slash peed over there on the floor"…

slid buttery snails and (blah)
Long Island Iced Teas

down her numb throat glued
her eyes on Billy Idol[2]

and Axl Rose[3] as they climbed
the spiral staircase (blah, blah) to the VIP lounge

She remembers Mickey Rourke[4]
that night swooping by (blah, blah) in

broad leathery gust
His bad boy swagger

always high and contrary
It was 1987, the year *Wild Orchid*[5]

came out, and she saw *Barfly*[6], told everyone (blah)
"That movie made me want to drink"

Fifteen years later she tries
to re-enact Faye Dunaway's[7] role

---

[2] During filming of the video "Eyes Without A Face," Billy was temporarily blinded when the heat of the set lights caused his contact lenses to fuse to his eyes.

[3] Axl said, "I discovered that I scream the same way whether I'm about to be devoured by a Great White or if a piece of seaweed touches my foot."

[4] Mickey Rourke claims Nicole Kidman ruined his film comeback. Kim Bassinger once called him "The Human Ashtray."

[5] Rourke and co-star Carré Otis were a couple while filming *Wild Orchid* and there is a persistent rumor that the sex scenes were not faked.

[6] Movie based on Charles Bukowski's life.

[7] Dunaway used to be married to Peter Wolf, leader of the J. Geils Band.

recites her favorite line (blah, blah, blah)
to strangers in Miami dives,

> "I don't hate people, (blah, blah) I just seem to feel better
> when they aren't around."

She meets Errol in a deserted beach bar
Named after Errol Flynn that

> swashbuckling womanizer (blah, blah)
> with his *Wicked, Wicked Ways*[8]

Back in the 80's Errol Flynn's
burned down mansion off Franklin street

> in Hollywood was a hangout (blah, blah)
> for punks who hiked up the steep

dirt path to the ruins of the house
gazed out over the city

> while chugging (blah, blah, blah)
> gallons of cheap red wine.

"My father use to work for Errol Flynn"
he says, "as caretaker on his yacht–*Zaca*[9].

> He's mentioned in the autobiography."
> She isn't sure whether (blah)

---

[8] Flynn autobiography, published posthumously in 1959. Rumored to be mostly made up, due to Flynn's confusion between his life and his films.
[9] Zaca means Peace in Samoan.

to believe him (blah, blah) since
she hasn't read the book

On the big screen Johnny Depp[10]
is believable (blah, blah, blah)

as a bad boy but she's not comfortable
with that, knows he's deep (blah)

and sensitive (blah) even though he
altered his *Winona[11] Forever* tattoo to

Wino Forever after their breakup (blah, blah)
Like *Six Degrees of Separation*[12]

it's connected:(blah) Errol on the beach and Errol Flynn,
Mickey Rourke and Johnny Depp

who both grew up in Florida (blah, blah) where
she lives now (blah, blah) with celluloid ghosts and heroes

tries to convince herself, (blah, blah, blah)
"It's just movies."

---

[10] "I had found the teachers, the soundtrack and the proper motivation for my life. Kerouac's train-of-thought writing style gave great inspiration for a train-of-thought existence – for better or for worse." From Johnny Depp's essay, *The Night I Met Allen Ginsberg: An appreciation of KEROUAC, BURROUGHS, CASSADY and the other bastards who ruined my life.*
[11] Winona Ryder and Depp dated on and off for four years. Ryder grew up on a commune in Northern California. Her godfather is LSD guru Timothy Leary.
[12] Researched by sociologists at Columbia University interested in what is known as "Small World Phenomenon." This is the idea that everyone in the world can be reached through a short chain of social acquaintances, but after more than thirty years, nobody knows if it's true.

WHEN I WAS IN LOVE

      Lust and the room grew
  small as zero.
            *

So I escaped everyday
to my silly restaurant job
watched Santo,
in the kitchen peeling shrimp,
extracting blue veins from flesh,
with the kind of grace
you lacked.
            *

      There's no salvation
      in distractions,
      only moments
      of "what ifs" driving me
      back to the ocean
      to search the seaweed
      and sewage
            *

      Clawless crabs, gull bones, syringes.

Blue bottle jellyfish, deflated
      like balloons the morning after a party.

I carry them home
set them on the bathroom sink next to the soap dish.

You don't want to touch them.

Ira Cohen

On Writing Poems

On Writing Poems

Every day I see the poem
which lies concealed in my
heart. If writing prolongs
                    solitude
it also brings about the encounter
with one's greatest need,
that ray of light, the beauty
which transforms
our identity into words
our very aspiration without
which we will be bereft
whether of dreams or divine
                        connection.

Jan. 26, 2006

Josh Davis

the glass being half empty

the glass being half empty

the glass being half empty,
i ordered another,
12 purple motherfuckers
on 16 jack and cokes
over 7 1/2 shots of tequila
and the portal back home
blind man,
something about a harp going out of tune,
and the prettiest girl in the room
pretending to be uptight and quiet
the second we blinked art
and made dead men smile

Mikey Delgado

There is about half a white moon tonight

The Standard

Sundays

at her first match

Queen and Country/Letter

There is about half a white moon tonight

There is about half a white moon tonight
against that exquisite blue the colour
of bottled ink. It sits over the bus shelter
by the all-night shop where boys will fight
later over drugs or girls. In the early morning
the unremitting boldness of a few drops
of some fool's blood pressed from his lips
by other lips, or by a fist without warning,
will look blue against the pavement stone,
and later as the sky lightens to its autumn white
some commuter may see these drops are shot
through like small red scattered leaves thrown
by an oracle from a cave, and that each leaf
is lettered with the story of itself.
I was lost in the sight of the moon.
The moon was beautiful, careless, and aloof.

The Standard

The readers of the Boston Evening Transcript
Sway in the wind like a field of ripe corn. - TS Eliot

Lucky them. My daughter's *madeleine*
will be the smell of fine dust in the long tunnels,
and the perching seats in the bright carriages
where readers of newspapers stumble
like thrown sheep as the brakes are applied
in a flourish of stopping and the train slows
into a thin tube of yellow platform light.

The doors slide and people tumble like damaged fruit
from burst boxes. Others take their places,
bewildered and dumb, done with duty, sleepwalking
to their stables and pens and batteries.
Cables are pulling us to pay-day,
to the early darkness of the suburbs,
to the dormitories above the paved-over fields.

LAST NIGHT'S DREAM CORRECTED   **39**

Sundays

Those men standing there on the chapel steps
in their staid suits, flanked by their quiet wives;
I wonder about the god they worship,
and their hard labour, and their dashed hopes.

The couples look so pale and joyless.
I wonder about their communion in the dark,
about the plangency of their crying out
for god, and their fingers clawing the air.

I wonder about the moment their backs
are arched, and whether they are young again then,
and graceful, and if they stare into each other's eyes
and cry out that they are burning with love.

And afterwards, about how they return to their bodies,
emptied of love, with their tongues stilled once more.

at her first match

for Trish

"oh come on referee!"
he jumps from his seat
and points. the steward
remonstrates, mentions

that Camus was a goalkeeper
and the crowd is a series
of waves and eruptions
and you must have sympathy

for existentialist footballers
who have arrived at their best
already, their greased hair
and shorts in frost-breath

January. oh the sun
bathed us for a while
and the crowd is as one
with its tentacles around

the yellow light-bathed
arena where some
may think
oh look at us!

at the football! baying!
we are an outpost
still of Rome,
paying for the spectacle,

unaware
in the twilight
of how night is falling
away from the contest,

how the darkness has crept
up to the walls of the sponsor's arena
while we were by the lit field,
listening to the thundering of feet.

Queen and Country/Letter

On Laughing Mushrooms we were,
all of us, except for
London Mikey the black boy,
and the lieutenant,
a posh cunt
on anti-depressants.

And patrolling out there
on the same street where
the guy who got killed two days before .
was in his house, in his coffin,
on the front room table,
and in the middle of his forehead
a tiny tiny blue bruise...
and I'm telling you now,
you wouldn't know he was dead,

you'd think the box was his bed
not that he'd gone down dead into the gutter
where twisted like that
he looked like he'd just got tired
of throwing stones
and had dropped down and curled up
and gone off to sleep,
not that one of us had shot the rubber bullet
straight at his Irish head
instead of into the ground in front of his feet.

And two days later down his street
the acid started to bubble through

as strong as ten bears
just as it all went twisted
like that bit where
at the end of *Bonnie and Clyde*
those birds get spooked
and all you can hear is flapping wings
and birds getting the fuck out of those trees
and they look at each other, Warren Beatty
and that blonde piece,
and you can see them thinking *what the fuck is this?*
this is fucking it...

and I don't know what did it to us that day,
perhaps a car backfired, or some cunt pulled a stunt
with a firework, but we hit the floor man
and shot up the fucking street with live fire,
right, left, and fucking centre.
And Dave from Swansea,
a big fat Swansea Jack bastard
was screaming *bandits! bandits! bandits!*
and everyone else screaming screaming screaming
about the fucking Pope and Irish cunts.
And where one minute that poor fucker was laid out
ready for the cemetery
in his Sunday best
looking like he'd had enough politics for one day
and had slipped into his box for a little sleep,
the next minute the lieutenant's screaming
hold your fire! hold your fucking fire!
screaming and bawling like a big fucking girl
whose dickhead boyfriend is being fucked-up
in the car park of a pub for being a twat;

and every window on the front of that guy's house
is shot to fuck, with us sticking our heads through there
from outer space,
like space cadets,
peering like vegetables
at the matchwood of the mashed up coffin
and the body with eleven rounds in it
tipped onto the floor,
ripped to big pieces,
covered in glass and fruit and a fucked up flag.

And we stared and stared at the squiggly wallpaper
cascading down the wall
like a waterfall,
and what we could see of the carpet pattern
was squirming
like a pit of snakes,
and you wouldn't believe the colours, as vivid
as the lieutenant's face, melting
like cartoon stuff.....and the silence man,
the absolute
fucking
silence.

And then transport came
and got us out of there
and everything was green
and everyone said
not to worry he was dead already
and now he looked it
and a couple of the boys said
ah fuck the acid;

and London Mikey the black boy
never came back
from his next leave.
Stabbed by a white boy
in a pub in cowboy country
south of the river. National Front.
Good fucking bloke he was, Mikey,
called his house his yard.
One of the boys, man.

Peace!

Later!

Stratos Fountoulis

Nostos

Nostos

Some divine moments in
fever of destiny, draw out
contrasts and aphorisms.
And they do insist.

*

A nostos of our dream shivers.
Wrapped in a song. At the first
turn, the song extinguishes, and...
Oh, yes.
Silence may provoke the world,
or Sorrow justice, but nostalgy of
the unknown had won us in our youth.
Immortality too, in a few joints.

*

And he, who has not wasted a
treasure in his youth may heal
that crack in the door.

*

As night falls, a woman's tender
whisper. It could be a farewell
to an age gone by. There is no
haste. There are no wagons
unloading any pirates of
pleasure. No.

*

I recall my first verse. A child then.
Eros-stricken by the faraway lights
and elders who slept on armchairs.
I would then enter a landscape,
painted on the oldest of our walls.

–Autumn was eternal there.

2003 Brussels

Kim Göransson

Nameless son of the south

Nameless son of the south

part one: my so-called childhood, indented

a slurp of tradition janks ox
   ygen into apologetic oxes, our daddy
in fields of green whom blisters
   pop, a portrait of
so fine and dandelion
a wife of the city
   before resurrection that holds
us indefinitely, with
exiled lips: rips us, devoids us
   we can see clearly mother rampage
her daily chores
and slumber, a slob in Mary's place
   come daddy night to pray
in gown so pretty
   the damned faggot had his
trousers lost, turn out the lights
and behold the end
of the metaphysical carnage

as it has us installed beforehand:
but now sleep, now triptych, now rattle
with doorlike passion
my sworn one

fleeting absolute and handsome
the Valery of our time, hand in purse
down stairway, into the worship puddle
   wipes tears from brow

wipes poem manhood mercy
that it is clearly she is a madame of sorts
    perhaps sailor with fuckable goldilocks
waiting on the bough to be
    touched:
    have you say accepted toast roasted your personal
salvation whipped with closure, into your
    mumbling heart
    have you gone yet nicely abroad
the underneath and seen
    so plenty the goose springs alike?

inclothed was she, so sneezed and ever
    mississippi flooded and yet
plunged by horizons, the cry of
some furniture dragged across
    a room, in the library
    she sat face forward, as happens
    when reading a book

there are posters of the revolution
now available in fur for our swedish friends
don't hesitate, it might be too late

part two: and by the sperm divided

the sentinels were prepared in glistening
sunlight, and ran free for a change
then castrated before they could see
and they saw what was unseen for many

fleeting also, down syrupy highways
cause, our reminiscent father figure

it came to a crossing, the promise
of a smile, fair lady tangled in locust
who spat fire, stirred blackbird and
wrote songs of a terrible beauty
all is stolen and kept hidden, even
zeus delightful on his bicycle, shouted

build us no more homes with chimney
mouth and asshole doorknob, please
i shall crush you to pebble and rock
with python arms and shape a circle
out of the dead and lead them across this
land of red, there is a bar up ahead

in the mind the great thinker sat
and plucked the grass with his toes
and looked up, upon which the mind
dangled, i see you have come a long
way, it is quite amazing how well
this grass tickles, i could laugh a loud

part three: boogie woogie, old fart

boogie woogie, old fart
i have loved much, and gained
many a pounds, sometimes
violet, sometimes blue
my cruelty has flowered and colored
even the frames, i paint no longer

in silence, but instead
into the bodies themselves,
it is all an illusion, familiar
faces falling as in pause
into the cracks, disappears-
so boogie woogie, shake
that thing, ruffle and drain
pray the leaf has you not
remembered, pray into the well
and well beyond, a paper boat
with big black holes to breathe through
might appear slightly sudden, paint dries
embarrassed by the skies that
cannot be cupped, drips
only when birthed, and birthed only once
a vibration, a voice
sentimental boogie woogie why sit here
all by your lonesome, with
your cock in hand, boogie woogie
meanwhile there might be a moment
up by the old mill, a sparkle
and burnt to the ground
boogie, i had a dream of this place-
i can't recall what comes next
woogie, oh woogie
i can't even remember where i put
my head, maybe this is what is meant
maybe this is what happens after
as a storm, we are folded and hunged
upsidedown, people walk around
looking all human saying things like
hello, how do you do
it's a very absent-minded painting
it's very you-
and you and you and you,

boogie woogie say who birthed these
soulful expressions?
boogie woogie is this the end
of the universe?
i have so many answers to question
oh no, oh boogie
kiss me- hold me tight
hold me tonight
woogie boogie

part four: the incomplete masterpiece

there's too much pressure
too much pressure
i could say
fingernail
nourishment
Palestine
flamingoes
hut
i could say
insolence
daft
chestnut
handkerchief
i could say
see you in Vienna!
look, a sand dollar!
dwarfs are funny
don't forget to
brush your teeth
but nothing

nothing
would really make any difference
anyhow

Susan Kennedy

It was the crow you see

Proper poems will not be written

It was the crow you see

For Lisa, Jo and Logan

It was the crow you see
black and shiny with his hood up
he passed the window as we ate
breakfast
strutting his crow stuff
could almost imagine him singing
you know - *Ki ooooora, Ki oooooora*
I'll be your dog
told her how I loved the crows
and her lips pursed the cigarette
vile, vicious thugs she said
they pick the eyeballs from the lambs
out in the fields
and I wondered where she got to knowing
about the cruelty of crows and
the gap in the middle of the rainbow
seemed to be pulling me towards some
hidden deeper meaning
only I couldn't quite grasp it
and her five year old dangled the feathery
tail of her pleat in the milk
skimming the cornflakes, sucked the milk off
and challenged us to scold her with
her eyes, which were brown, like her fathers
who lived near the fields, where the lambs
risked their vision on a daily basis
and my baby, who's really no longer a baby
turned and said, *I love the crows too Mum*
but I love the lambs more
and in my head there was a matt photo finish

of the lambs in the fields, lying on the grass, with
black holes, where their eyes should be
and flies, and I looked around the table
at the lambs, all three of them
and suddenly
I feared the crows

10/9/02

Proper poems will not be written

Proper poems will not be written
by the uneducated
for the grammar will not stand up
to the severe beatings
it will receive
once exposed
to the educated masses.

Proper poems will not be written
by the ordinary shopworker
for her ideas and dreams
are dull and of course
ordinary,
they will fail the tests
set by the exam boards
whose rulings
set in stone
must be obeyed.

Proper poetry will not be written
by housewives or mothers
left at home, for hours on end
while their men do the real work
and bring home the money
to pay for the paper
and ink
necessary for the poet
to breathe.

Proper poetry will not be written
by the woman who stands
alone on the top of the hill

remembering, way back
when,
the woman who can still hear
the voices and see the faces
of the long dead,
the dead, and feel the breath
of the dying
on her neck.

Proper poetry will not be written
by me, or you
for poems cannot be forced
into existence,
they are kissed into life
by heartbroken lovers,
bereaved fathers,
lost children and those
who remember
the bodies of the dead,
so many bodies
that there is no earth
as far as the eye can see.

Proper poetry is not written
it fights its way into being
through the mouth of the poet,
his wet, hot mouth
the womb,
his black charcoal pencil
the incubator,
it fights its way from the bowels
of the earths misery
it fights its way from the heights
of the heavens joys

and sets itself upon the pages
of the poets heart.

16/10/02

Joanne Kyger

Dust

The Fog is Halfway Over the Mesa

DUST

It's terrible what's happening in this war atmosphere
    when 'your' government lies
        to you and neglects the people

It's bad for your mind when the politics of connection
    show ignorance and preference
        for the stupid junta
            that has slyly pre-empted the beehive

Time to dive for the Madhayamika school
    and middle way ourselves
        through the course of the oppression to come
        phew!

I'd prefer not to have to bother
    in this landscape of spring to judge
        whether these apple blossom branches
        are natural or not
            I just want to be ordinary
            and finish my toast

While Arthur Okamura is on the prowl
    with his notebook and pen
        sketching the dust
        in the wind

                May 15, 2003

THE FOG IS HALFWAY OVER THE MESA

My table of life for the past
thirty years or so is not broken
up into incidents as much as continuum

So much for the skill of living
the outer life of season
while the 'inner' buttress
certainly becomes no wiser

Have you heard this a thousand times before
from anybody & everybody

And that's it? Except you allow
the rapid combine of elements
heretofore disparate: like Bodhidharma cruising
the Pacifica as a   surfboarding Coyote
and the poor bonged-on-head disciple Naropa
here to meet him
along with the classic
Greco-Roman education
that always hauls Odysseus along
–probably the oldest of the lot

but none of it 'indigenous' to here except
through conviction of the poet   combining

these strands into a useful cord,   a thread

to throw into the dream and see it
come up clear
as a picture in the evening

August 3, 2000

Elias Miller

death brings different socks

God the Stepfather

death brings different socks

bilirubin makes up for your lack of asian genes
as the sunlight writes your name in shadows
now made more even as breathing slows
or as thinking slows.
who knows?

closets full of unworn clothes
compete for space as we cram ourselves
between drawers of tube socks and the leaky loo
twelve years a bachelor marked out in chilli cans and condensed
soup
finally you've flown the coup
and women flock to clean up after you.

your youngest son builds the box
(which we wipe down with your socks)
and your oldest waits for you to look with recognition
but by your own admission
you lived for years waiting to be seen
as you hid on Sand road behind the cedar hedge
with the radio always on in case the world ended without you

they say that death comes with a rattle
but it sounded more like socks stuffed in a box
and the muffled sense of loss
that comes when you give away something you never really had

though we plan to bury you
to the sound of taps under a triangular flag
we bury the memories of all we missed
the dad that came and left but liked to hover
like an aloof eagle in the sky

occasionally swooping before he said goodbye.

26/4/04

God the Stepfather

"I have two fathers
Two Gods
One dead and the other dying
Part of one whole
The stepfather, the son, and the only ghost."

He came into my life unbidden
Moving carefully so as not to disturb my toys
And like Zeus seduced my mother while I slept.

He spent time talking to me about school,
About logic and perspective
And I could see how His beard covered pock marks.
His youth let Him down,
And He needed to conceal it.

The times He pressed his lips until white
(and the strike seemed not far behind)
I hid in His old Thunderbird
Parked in the garage next to the stacks of old Playboys.

His own son visited,
Sometimes a Tom and others a Thomas,
He was the first to show me a centerfold
Wearing nothing but a pink sunhat and red platform shoes
Pink nipples and orange pubes.
I didn't understand why he left his door ajar
And spent Saturday mornings under his covers
He wanted us to play make believe
Where he was the queen and I was the subject.
He asked me for worship from my mouth

And I couldn't.
I wasn't his servant.

My mother wanted more than me
Because my father gave her four (and she lost three)
But she wouldn't take what Stepfather had
At age nine, I visited her in the ward.
Her barren womb removed,
He couldn't make her whole.

He used to give me commands
And taught me right from wrong
But mostly I saw He lived above His law.
He trained me to hate what He hated
And hate what He loved
And I learned.
I ate like He did.
I ate to escape.
And I rebelled
Quietly

I followed a doctrine
Dictated by guts and genitals
Sentimental and penitent
Pleasing the strongest impulses to surface
Always unable to numb desire.
Like an oil fire
My smoke filled the sky

He gets older powers fading
Faster now that my dad is gone
Ineffable and ineffectual
Slowing and swerving
Clinging to the steering wheel.

And I see my end in His end
I see my eyes in His
The dusty books in wooden shelves
Discarded tools filling the workshop
Boxes of memories among the rats
Eaten slowly, growing holes,
His reason stolen by the gnaw of hours.

The house He built needs care
Mother waits for Him
She knows where He is
And He knows why
But will He pass below her
Under the bricks and concrete His hands have touched
Into the rest that waits like hole
Sucking at Him until He's small enough to swallow
Leaving His ghost to keep her thoughts warm

I'd ask Him for forgiveness
But He'd just make excuses,
His behaviour beyond reproach
Outline burned like a shadow
Face glowing in the cathode light
Clicking away the moments that remain.

20/9/04

Stephen Moran

Ballad

Ballad

It is the hour of waking alone.
Two jets are unzipping the sky.
Boxwood hedges await me
and watch my feet go by.

The pines are hiding their scent
with the privet for tonight.
They hold no interest this morning,
enervated by so much light.

The dead grocer is still alive,
surly, serving in the shop,
henpecked in a biscuit coat
at the parade where buses stop.

Joan Gentle is near me now
worth marrying just for the name.
She often gets on the sixteen,
but she is dead just the same.

Two friends linking arms as always
on the path by the flower bed
will never get to hear about TaTu,
Aids or crack, because they're dead.

The conductor with nothing to say
still hears the sister squeal
"That's my brother, that's my brother!"
He too has passed under the wheel.

Maisie of the hotpants is a zombie
in the kiosk selling cigarettes

and I still buy ten Senior Service
and inhale without any regrets.

There's where Vicky lives over the shop.
She cuts hair and makes mothers blonde.
They still share tea and drink gossip
even though they're beyond the beyond.

Their blueprints are filed under gone
missing, and presumed unknown.
Although we are dead, we're alive -
all in the hour of waking alone.

Julie Payne

a window for optimism

a window for optimism

animals get lucky
out there where the tinkling windchimes decide the tone
a length of lace won't change it
there is nothing wrong with the window I should not worry about
the curtain

if it ever gets warm
I will open the thing and scream
from the highest point in my dirty lungs
won't you be my fucking neighbor

the dog needs an orgasm she can't help it
she has no one to touch that spot
except the cat and the cat
is uncooperative

I am a cul-de-sac soul
a semi-circle of open doors
transplanted in the middle of a squared block
surrounded by rectangles

some people do not adjust to loss
I like to walk when I lose my keys
there are seventy-nine reasons why I can't be your girl
just one why I should

walking the dog was once a hello how do you do
type of thing, a gee your yard looks nice
how's the hydrangea, did you ever
fix that lawnmower or find the tip of that finger

the cat howls again from the basement, tattle-tales
stop this fucking
dog
right meow

I want to go home
where the lavender walls were warm
where circles were safe
windows stayed open well into autumn

sweeping the kitchen floor I think
humans are all so unaware
so many tiny little universes disevolved
moving from places that should not be left

this is my moment
the one I don't talk about
where I know and I know and I know
and there is nothing I can do but continue to know

the thing that is right
the thing that should be done but isn't
is out there where animals know more
and they don't get it right either

there's a storm coming in
the curtains wave their flags in surrender
and will soon let go from the broken rod
I refuse I refuse I refuse

to close the thing again

Michael Rothenberg

Waiting for Venus to die

Grasshopper

Éire

WAITING FOR VENUS TO DIE

More food, more sleep, no excuses

Baby beaten to death because it cries
Twins abandoned before New Year

Is she an astral lover or holy song?

Don't take my dramas, she says
They're all I have!

Morning heat bends the blinds
Bay shimmers and sparks

Look at me, I'm naked!
Composed in my chair

Listen as tears flash and smolder

Dear She-Ones!
Embrace me in attentiveness
Nubile daughters come with bright eyes
Surround my bed silently, please
Don't wait until I've entirely dissolved
I'm just beginning to like myself

I want to be treasured by a woman

An orgiastic mini-series, bed to bed
That's how it happened, fixation
Became criminal
Seed spread complex and legend

Still penetrating eyes
Pale quivering lips. Thighs
Wrapped about thighs. Out of breath
Clenching my neck without forgiveness

Maybe it comes back around
After the flesh is cut away
A fish swims from the wall

Somethings mean something
Somethings sweet nothings

Listen to this

Christmas morning
Call me, call!
Bells in my head
I become invisible

Christmas morning
I run away for a few hours
Time marches on
What the hell!
I'm living for myself
Waiting for Venus to die!

Ocean Drive
Candy-colored Deco motel row
Babes in black leotards roller-blade

Afternoon drizzle

Gray velvet doomsday stillness
Sugar cane burning haze

New Years Eve
Antipasto of sliced veal, white beans

Sign of continuing music and grace
Flares, fireworks, random gunfire

I didn't know she loved me
Years later she returned
Masquerading as another
Woman. I touched her face

Shell of a woman

By the swimming pool
Dark clouds. Tropic winds blow cold through
Luxuriant fronds

A naked man clutches a pink flamingo

12/22/95
Florida

GRASSHOPPER
            for Erika

Lately I fear I'll die, suddenly, at a critical time
In my career, outside of history

            And she will know

I've always loved her
blighted palms, coral ruins

Blood-shapely artifacts, lightning
Pasted on black sky, high-rise hotels

            Teeth in salt-worn jaw
            clamped on a planetary skyline

            Tragic city!
You love everyone but can't live with yourself

Dozing under clouded weight of a gray storm
Hammers pummel concrete
into limestone graves

There goes the ghost
of the man who was my doctor

Bouquets scream with summer's melting petals

            Miami
            July 16, 1997

ÉIRE

"We are told how in the beginning it came to pass that like
cabbaging Cincinnatus the grand old gardener was saving daylight
under his redwood tree one sultry sabbath afternoon…"
Finnegans Wake, James Joyce

*

Desire's siren reams my cock
Locked up inside
Don't block me

with obligations, paperwork
and physical fitness
Death comes soon enough

Listless Assistant
use these words even if
they don't come naturally

Even if you wouldn't
ordinarily use them
Close the drapes

Draw the blinds
It's the same thing
Come to bed

*

Duke of Wellington
Beef Wellington

Duke Ellington
Liffey Bridge

Metal Bridge
1816 Ha'penny Bridge

1919 no penny bridge
Restored w/ original period lamps

*

Uileann pipes
Guinness Stout
Cobbled streets of Temple Bar
Ireland's Eye, Book of Kells
Beef and cabbage
At the train station looking for The Perfect Poem

*

Pelicans, puffins, cormorants
Gulls warning overhead
Climb rock & bracken of Ireland's Eye

Howth Festival music and dance
"Be kind to your web-footed friends"

Tourists clutter graveyards

Swirled ice cream cones and tasseled belly buttons

*

Book of Kells

2 sausages 6 sugar donuts
Platter of lamb & rice

"A cynic knows the price of things and not the value"

James Joyce's bedroom
recreated in National Library

"Where ordinary things wear lovely wings"

The oldest harp in Ireland
Indigestion

*

Vikings, long boats, mummies
Gold, silver, bone

Jeweled shrine of sacred texts
Burial urns, bog body

Mortuary of killed weapons
Quest for quotidian

Crystal, stone, Roman sarcophagi
Rules, wars, conquests

Invasions
George Bush, Tony Blair

*

I swear I saw Cosmos
with rap music headphones
reading Ulysses without a map

*

Duck on a rugby field
What happened to the great
historical fragments?

"Take a seat, Love"

Chocolate fudge, French fries
Doritos, orange sherbet
Here or in Canada
The Cosmos bus. Mystery Train

Oh Muse repair my broken verse!

"Tractors descend upon the Peninsula"
??Railtown??

The Cooley Mountains
Carlingford Lough overlooking
Mountains of Mourne
Land of The Tain

Poems on the window

*

"Fresh Fish, Love?"

*

Connolly Station, 1:34 pm, platform 3

Drum; golf clubs, mothers & babies
Tracks, trestles, creaking, rattling

What rough beast slouching toward Innisfree

*

"If you haven't been west of the Shannon
you haven't been to Ireland"

*

"Cigarettes Kill"
"Babies become missiles"

*

"An extraordinary risk of ordinary things"

*

Holly, jellyfish, seaweed, mushrooms

Cows in the ocean
Sheep in the dunes

*

Wild red fuchsia, heather
Salmon falls, Georgian renovations
Doe Castle, flat tire, Irish speaking
people, Corncutter's Pub, stone bridge
starfish, anemone, political positions
What's the difference between Irish
living in Ireland & 40 million,
first or second generation in USA?
Many say they hate Bush
So why don't they tell their
relatives in New Bethlehem to vote
him off his stolen throne
No need for kings in Washington, D.C.
Barnacles baked beans
When they heard I was going to Ireland
someone said, "Don't do anything
you don't want to do" Is that possible?
chatter of teeming ecology. Wild Irish roses
mussels, chips, lamb...

*

Lilies, begonias, geranium, mums

Cosmos wants to touch everything, scale castle wall
Capture enormous, belittle sensible
Embrace lovable

Pathos, bathos, ethos
Imbue tercet

A life spent looking for precious rocks & shells
on a magic beach. Take them home
A week later they're vaguely memorable

                                *

Ramelton, Atlantic Drive

                                *

Swilley river
Walk by McDaid's bottling plant

Leave glasses in room at B & B
Starlings crow

                                *

Bed sinks in the middle

A troubled girl
Been like this all her life, she says

All I want to do is get away
from death & repetition

Starlings crow

*

"Have a nice day, Love"
        Black face ship, Glenveigh Castle, seashell
studded walls, white marble stag's heads
        (still life/ still born)

*

Wake 3 hours early
Walk in garden with Terri
Gray tits, blue tits, tuberous begonia
Sweet pea, lilies, white fuchsia, blue
Hydrangea leeks, cabbage, mint

Finches at bird feeder
    Gold fish in tinkling pond

Strawberries, raspberries, buddleia
Purple and red fuchsia, bees
Hot house tomatoes
Ferns, grasses, nasturtium

A stuffed owl guards the sun room

Pissy, moody, exhilarated
Scones & cream

Romanian Roy Orbison sings
between department stores and pubs

"It's Now Or Never"

I learn there's nothing I can say
without getting her angry

I stop speaking
which only angers her more

Between Modern Art Museum and Kilmainham Gaol
Signs: Hedgehog, Sheep, Cat

Body snatchers in Bully's Acre

    Guinness Brewery
       Statue of Molly Malone
  St. Patrick's Church
      Writer's Museum
      Where James Joyce met his wife

Loiterers outside Brogan's Pub
speak in poetry

River Liffey, or Gulfstream
flows its own verse

Madness of the Modern world
    Priests in wars in one green republic
    Keep god's swords sharp and piercing
     for a thousand years

            "Ulysses on The Cross"

    Potatoes fail, millions die

Scriptures, serpents, clover

dean strom

i'm disappointyheaded

The Dumbstruck Tone of K Baffled Asterisk*

drenched

i'm disappointyheaded

i'm disappointyheaded none of you critics pointed out the superfluity of our times. superfluity has a way of fixing itself to my doorknob which falls off when i sleep. there are 10 billion new ways of throwing fruit at the actors but only one you. you're unique. you're the only unique thing in the universe. everything else has been multiplicated and put into a storage chamber, whose space is through expanding if they can't find new ways to compress things. my mother, who cooks new dishes everyday, remarked on the ephemeral nature of crockery and that she can't find her good pots anymore - even while she knows they're there. i pluck nose hairs. on turtle day i try to get my friend spencer to do my chores. it takes him a long time to recognize my voice when i call him from the bottom of turtle bay. i usually surface right about noon. it's later in the evening when we get together for shadow puppeteering. my fingers on the wall resemble tendrils on a sponge. his look like a dog made out of balloons unfocused due to inadequate screen resolution. fortune smiles down like a crescent moon, wavy on the water's surface. but suffering is just another way of selling canned goods.

i'm shellshockedamazed you are here relatively unscathed. your skin doesn't drip from your body. your armor doesn't sting my eyes. your horse is quite spectacular and i'd like to be in your employ. i'm pleading to be heard like the explosion whose resistance was futile and the carnival barkers drunk. after the noon glory there will be camel races and a ponce de leon theme party. i'm pretty sure they're holding a wake in the wee wee hours of the t.v. glimmering. but you're unique. you sit above it all because you have the garden club card and the unique way of acknowledging spring. the you part of you can't be bought or sold no matter how much the clever exchange's current rate - how much of the piggy the market ate. i'm relying on you to tell the universe which way to expand and i'm trying to shine under your example.

spencer never gets home before five midgets on a mission suddenly revoke the circumstances which got them there. it was not likely they could be recognized but the possibility of being stabbed in the heart by a dagger is staggering to the drunk one who is merely trying to steal some peace out of the city in order to reacquaint himself to the nice people who give him things. he comes upon spencer and there is a slight shocked pause, as i heard it described, and each of them went their separate ways with the feeling of a missed opportunity.

fate is a feckle furlough when all you have to offer has left for finishing school and quit brushing its teeth. at least so i imagine, sitting on my toadstool waiting for devolution to finally reveal its recipe for creme brulee. there are many things to think about here but none of them are unthought or arranged in such a way as to remind me of my former lives as told to me by some old hag i couldn't truss up in truth armor and drown to see if she was real.

sometimes you just gotta sing along. sometimes there ain't nothing better than ink drying on an old cotton sleeve - when there was no paper available - that day back in the civil war when the rebel Johan Jan Van de Javel wore it proudly until he was slowly dying without morphine to soothe him and he suddenly had something to say to his one true love who, unknown to him, had already left him for the yankee captain who shot one mr. Johan Jan Van de Javel and who subsequently left Johan's one true love for glory and death with his good friend General George Armstrong Custer. it was the perfect triangle as seen from a distance of seven trillion light years away when that kind of distance allows the observer to not have much feeling for the poor souls as they might have been called in another time. another place.

it's been told, or so i have heard, that when everybody finally feels the rush of realization the drains of freedom will clear their pipes all the way to their exit in an alternate universe, one devoid of reason or care. it's been asserted through my very ears that one Felix Nolstalga of Wilsaukie Misconsin has won a very fine dead ermine to give to his wife of some 30 years. forever. and ever. and ever.

The Dumbstruck Tone of K Baffled Asterisk*

LET us give up then, you and me,
When the dawn tattered flag of infinity
Flies like a corpse at Thanksgiving;
Let us give up, admit the desert alleys,
The clattering machine gun
Of relentless unreflecting ideology
And sawtoothed kosher deceits in Tel Aviv:
Treats that follow like a mutual agreement
Of the Bible's Revelations
Lead us into a self fulfilling prophesy
Oh, do not ask, What time it be?
Let us embrace our insanity.

In the gloom the children run and play
Only having yesterday.

The yellow dog that scratches its back upon the rubbish heap,
The acrid cur that rubs its muzzle on the whole damned keep
Licked its tongue into the bronchi of the lungs,
Lingered upon the bulges of lividity,
Let dribble upon its mange maggots that fell from its teeth,
Stumbled by the doorstep, took a last breath,
And seeing that it was a final November night,
Curled once around the welcome mat and closed its eyes.

so much to dread
Upon

a dead sea
scroll

teared with dumb
desire

inside a hermetic
seal.

I saw the narrow minds of my generation deceived by government,
shrieking hysterically; lies dragging us through shit in the
illumination of a television screen; foxnewsed squareshirts
nattering the mythologies of the day, seduced by the machinery of
war, nattily attired in bow ties, hollow-cheeked but sat-up straight
in the supernatural whizbang of sound effects and graphics floating
across their membranes. They bared their teeth for Hannity with
the belief that hell is a Hollywood staging of homosexual school
teachers who passed through universities hallucinating on LSD and
atheist dogma and lay amongst the scum of liberality and should
be expunged from the earth in a fiery destruction for printing
abominations above the noses of the righteous and for glowering
and burning their mocking poems into our misery weakly allowing
terroreratorists to attack us in our underwear.

* Apologies to T.S. Eliot, William Carlos Williams, and Allen
Ginsberg.

drenched

leaves
drip
dirty
from the top of the tree

and splash around the children
nursery rhyming.

if they're lucky they'll stay dry this year
and tear up clovers but nevermind
the voice from the school house
jangling lessons.

and then the sophisticated television
in images
snappy and vile
promises pointless futures of greed and politics.

this year the children are all getting drenched.
let's follow one child now
as he grows through the peaceful anatomy of lizards
and fantasy
on his gameboy screen.
don't be too quick to tell him
beyond the flying dragons
is nothing but a dying planet and a corporation
sponsoring it.
but don't let him discover it all on his own either
or he'll never get home again.

blem vide

Art Without Instructions (an art disclaimer)

Art Without Instructions (an art disclaimer)

Not all art is well thought-out, I think
art is a survivor of love thrown in the trash
to avoid explaining what 'sunshine echo' means
art is your trash
trash is a round table
do not forget that, folks
art isn't trash
and trash is a round table
art is a round table

a round table is a
psychological symbol of trash
art is a recycled telephone book

"how is art a recycled telephone book? are you being sarcastic?"

art is 2 parts iodine & 3 parts warm urine

"are you putting me on? is this automatic free-association?"

have you noticed the CIA in association?

"well, yes, now that you mention it,
I do see the CIA in association"

fool,
art is the ASS
in association
not the CIA
okay?
art may be trash
but trash isn't necessarily art

art is perfectly casual
smooth as astro glide
universe & space-time
is causal not casual
art laughs at me sounding smart
as if by accident (and not fraud)

again, art is an accident

art can be
textually appalling
or art can come calling
your name in divorce court
art can be the west nile virus, orange alerts,
security checks, snipers, honest comets,
four quartets, fascist ashes, or a modest
recycle bin laden caveman
boo!
art could be a gay pirate dressed up
as a ditzy blonde in g-string
and you'd have no control over it
get over it
art can be the result
of years effort
or a gimmicky toss-off

or art can come from
feeling sick
and banging on keys
art is perfectly casual
just as usual
even if you spell it
against power
In art as in life – be just.
But if you cannot be just – be arbitrary.

Just relax
act casual
yes, art is
perfectly agile
art is a smashed atom
art is naturally irrational
art is smooth, not obvious
or very obvious
perfectly casual
just as usual
by the way,
if you're comfortable
you're wrong

art spies on you

you are being watched
and described
not always in a flattering way
smile if you need instructions
(and if you're smiling now, you owe me lunch)

Richard Wright

Poems that need no introduction

1. The Introduction

Poems that need no introduction

1. The Introduction

At The Reading, we get the soft drinks first
– before they open the real, the harder stuff –
They Introduce: the who and where and when
and, surprisingly often, tell us the why.

I'd like to write this poem so that it needs
no codebook, no crib to the decryption,
no rosetta stone to break the ideograms
into something approaching the intelligible.

I'd like you and this poem to bump into each other
like total strangers meeting at a corner,
too suddenly, and one knocked down, and one who picks
the other up and then tells him the story of his life.

Just then and there and totally, as you walk along
and beat the dust from off your trouser legs.

I always liked the introductions best.
That's where you get the little bit of laugh,
if any. And modesty shows through – if any, again.
And what it's all about – if anything.

If there is anything the Poet can say besides
'I had to write this stuff' he says it then
– she says it then – gives us the spiel
and after, after the communication, you get the poem.

I'd like to write this poem so that it needs
no-one to introduce The Poem to you.

It just walks up and shakes you by the hand
all by itself and you know what it is,

because it sits right there in front of you,
and isn't any more – or any less –
than what you see.
That's what I'd like to do.

Contributors

Raewyn Alexander is a novelist, poet, fine cook of peasant proportions, publisher, communicator, arts advocate and non-fiction writer despite trying to escape to strategic analyst, editor of Magazine, a literary annual (bright_com@xtra.co.nz).

Richard Atkinson is a poet of Newcastle-Upon-Tyne.

Bill Berkson is the author of sixteen books and pamphlets of poetry, including the recent collections *Serenade* and *Fugue State* and a volume of his 1960s collaborations with Frank O'Hara, *Hymns of St. Bridget & Other Writings*. Most recently, Arion Press has published *Gloria*, a set of new poems accompanied by etchings by Alex Katz. A selection of his criticism, *The Sweet Singer of Modernism & Other Art Writings 1985-2003*, appeared from Qua Books in 2004. He was the Distinguished Mellon Lecturer for 2006 at the Skowhegan School of Art. He lives in San Francisco.

J. Tyler Blue lives in Baltimore. He likes things. Many things. Even carrots. He is author of a collection of poetry and short fiction, "The Baltimore Years".

Sean Brijbasi collects words from the infralittoral zone where waves of poetry break onto the shore of prose. (It has been said by somebody.) He is the author of two books, "One Note Symphonies" and "Still Life in Motion".

Terri Carrion was conceived in Venezuela and born in New York to a Galician mother and a Cuban Father. She has lived in Los Angeles and Miami and currently nests in Northern California among the redwoods. Terri Carrion is the assistant editor of Big Bridge an online magazine of poetry, art and everything else. Her own poetry and photography has appeared and disappeared in various publications.

Ira Cohen is the author of Poems from the Akashic Record and maker of the film Kings with Straw Mats. He is known around the world for his poems, his photographs, his films, and his recordings. He published the famous magazine Gnaoua in Morocco. His life is a magic carpet.

Josh Davis is a prolific writer and part-time rock god. He is working on his third novel "Under the Blue Banner of Heaven".

Mikey Delgado didn't serve in the navy or attend university and is not drawn to Germanic folklore yet.

Stratos Fountoulis is a full-time visual artist with over 85 solo and group shows. Living and working between Athens, Greece and Brussels, Belgium. Grew up in South Africa. His work is found in many public and corporate collections in Europe and the US. Although he's published mainly poetic passages in literary reviews, he does not consider himself a writer. He says that by writing, he is only confessing his eternal immaturity to Aristophanes.

Kim Göransson was born in Umeå, Sweden in 1982. He moved to the United States in 2005 and currently lives in Danville, VA.

Susan Kennedy lives in the north of Scotland where she moonlights in the poetry mines.

Joanne Kyger is a Foundation for Contemporary Arts 2005 and 2006 Grant Recipient. A native Californian, she teaches at new College of California in San Francisco and in the Poetics Program at the Naropa Institute in Boulder, Colorado. Joanne Kyger has published over 20 books of poetry. She was the winner of the National Poetry Series in 1983 for her book Going On. Her most recent books of poems include God Never Dies (Blue Press), The Distressed Look (Coyote Books), Again (La Alameda Press), and As Ever: Selected Poems published by Penguin Books.

Elias Miller was born in Steinbeck's town. He got lost at an impressionable age in the barren wilds of Berkeley but saved up and escaped to the bright lights and sophistication of Australia and the former Soviet Union. He says he had to start writing poetry when the money ran out. These days he is a prolific poet and screenwriter. He works and lives in Puget Sound, northwestern Washingon with his wife and two children.

Stephen Moran is from Dublin originally and from London unoriginally. He would like to be a highly paid amateur and confound his creditors. Yes, confound them. He has one book of short stories out, "The London Silence." He also contributes to a number of websites, including his own www.stephenmoran.net.

Julie Payne hangs out in Bettendorf, Iowa and doesn't do anything except avoid high winds. She doesn't believe in submission.

Michael Rothenberg has been an active environmentalist in the San Francisco Bay Area for the past 25 years. His books of poems include The Paris Journals (Fish Drum), Monk Daddy (Blue Press) and Unhurried Vision (La Alameda Press). Rothenberg is editor and publisher of Big Bridge, www.bigbridge.org. He is also editor of Overtime, Selected Poems by Philip Whalen (Penguin), As Ever, Selected Poems by Joanne Kyger (Penguin) and David's Copy, Selected Poems by David Meltzer. He is presently working on the selected poems of Edward Dorn (Penguin, 2007) and the Collected Poems of Philip Whalen (Wesleyan University Press, 2007).

Dean Strom would never want to admit that anything we wrote about him is true. He was once observed nearly objectively using a new process called rebound-effect2 but there was 1 dissenter out of 107. Think how many that is out of 6,502,938,629, latest world population estimate 10:09 GMT (EST USA+5) Mar 12, 2006.

Blem Vide is an under funded self-scrutinizing word factory whose main job has been poetry management for the cryptic Babble On to Babylon art project exploding together over the desk of Adam the Atomic Scribbler of Curious Notes.

Richard Wright

Other books from Pretend Genius Press

still life in motion by **sean brijbasi**
isbn: 0974726109

the muse and the mechanism by **josh davis**
isbn: 0974726176

dancing the maze by **kenneth dawson**
isbn: 0974726192

the london silence by **stephen moran**
isbn: 0974726141

nothing will save you by **dean strom**
isbn: 0974726117

babble on to babylon by **blem vide**
isbn: 0974726184

fish drink like us an anthology of fiction
isbn: 097785261X

Available from all good booksellers

www.pretendgenius.com

www.ingramcontent.com/pod-product-compliance
Lightning Source LLC
Chambersburg PA
CBHW051837040426
42447CB00006B/569